SHORT WAL

Essex

Other areas covered in the Pub Walks series include:

Bedfordshire
Berkshire
Birmingham & Coventry
Bournemouth & Poole
Bristol and Bath
Buckinghamshire
Cambridgeshire
Cheshire
The Chilterns
The Cotswolds
The Cotswold Way
County Durham
North & West Cumbria
South Cumbria
Dartmoor & South Devon
Derbyshire
Essex
West Essex
Exmoor & North Devon
Gloucestershire
Herefordshire
Hertfordshire
The Icknield Way Path
The Isle of Wight
Lancashire
Leicestershire and Rutland

Lincolnshire
North London
Middlesex & West London
Midshires Way – Northern Section
Midshires Way – Southern Section
Norfolk
Northamptonshire
Nottinghamshire
Oxfordshire
Shropshire
Staffordshire
Suffolk
Surrey
The Surrey Hills
The Thames Valley
North Wales
South Wales
Warwickshire
Wayfarer's Walk
Wiltshire
Worcestershire
Wye Valley & Forest of Dean
East Yorkshire
North Yorkshire
South Yorkshire
West Yorkshire

A complete catalogue is available from the publisher at
3 Catherine Road, Newbury, Berkshire.

SHORT WALKS FROM
Essex Pubs

Norman Skinner

COUNTRYSIDE BOOKS
NEWBURY, BERKSHIRE

COUNTRYSIDE BOOKS
3 Catherine Road
Newbury, Berkshire

ISBN 1 85306 410 6

Designed by Mon Mohan
Cover illustration by Colin Doggett
Photographs and maps by Ann Skinner

Produced through MRM Associates Ltd., Reading
Typeset by Paragon Typesetters, Newton-le-Willows
Printed by Woolnough Bookbinding Ltd., Irthlingborough

Contents

Publisher's Note

We hope that you obtain considerable enjoyment from this book; great care has been taken in its preparation. However, changes of landlord and actual closures are sadly not uncommon. Likewise, although at the time of publication all routes followed public rights of way or permitted paths, diversion orders can be made and permissions withdrawn.

We cannot of course be held responsible for such diversion orders and any inaccuracies in the text which result from these or any other changes to the routes nor any damage which might result from walkers trespassing on private property. We are anxious though that all details covering the walks and the pubs are kept up to date and would therefore welcome information from readers which would be relevant to future editions.

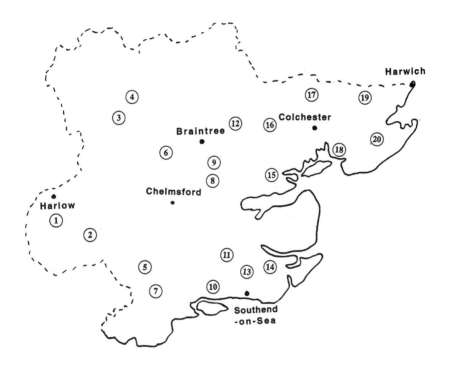

Area map showing locations of the walks.

Introduction

I am delighted to have had another opportunity to write about the Essex countryside and to link some fine pubs with some superb short walks. At these pubs, there is always good liquid refreshment on offer and, more often than not, inexpensive and nourishing food. The walks provide a chance to fully explore the county. A few are quite close to major towns such as Harlow, Colchester and Southend-on-Sea. Others are further afield, deep in the interior of rural Essex.

In the last ten years, walking has become an increasingly popular pastime. I would like to believe that authors like me, and publishers such as Countryside Books, have played a not insubstantial part in this process. The 1990 Rights of Way Act has provided ample encouragement to county highway departments, and to landowners, to greatly improve the condition of our paths. Locally, both these parties have been assisted by the Essex Area Ramblers' Association.

For those who have taken up pub walks regularly, through reading my books, and especially newcomers to the walking fold, I commend this selection of walks and pubs. I hope you will have the same enjoyment using the book as my wife Ann and I have had in preparing it.

It is well worth carrying the Ordnance Survey map relevant to each walk. The map numbers are indicated for each chapter in the *Length of the walk* sections. These can usually be borrowed from public libraries. The sketch maps are based on my own local surveys and although not to scale, they should prove a considerable aid to route finding.

It is clear that walking, as well as being extremely enjoyable, is also very good for you. However, dressing for the weather is no different when walking in the countryside than in any other outdoor activity; so if showery conditions are forecast, it is as well to carry a light waterproof. Footwear can be varied with the weather from trainers to leather boots, as you deem appropriate, but some conditions will dictate the use of wellington boots. Do remember, however, when going into a pub after the walk, to wear boot covers or change into 'mud-free' footwear, which can be kept in the car boot.

Parking at the pub for any reason other than as a patron of the inn, can be a source of friction between the pub staff and the visitor. Where space is available and at almost all the establishments featured in this book, you are welcome to park your car while you complete these walks. If you decide to walk during opening hours, but before you visit the pub, you would be well advised to make yourself known to the bar staff and obtain permission from them before you depart for your walk. If you are making an early start and intending to visit the pub on your return, then a telephone call to the pub would be a good idea – but please remember that keeping a pub involves working unsocial hours and a 7 am phone call from a bright, 'booted' walker will not be appreciated! If you just want to use the pub as a start/finish point or as a rendezvous, and are not intending to visit the pub, please do not use the pub car park.

I would like to pay a special tribute to my wife, who produced all the maps as well as the photographs for the book. On numerous occasions, she accompanied me on my field trips and I am extremely grateful for her encouragement with all the preparations.

Norman Skinner
Summer 1996

① Hastingwood
The Rainbow and Dove

Hastingwood and its common are still of a charmingly rural nature despite the presence of the M11 and the proximity of Harlow. The pub, which was once a farmhouse, was created to assist with the changing of horses on the Norwich to London coach. Originally known as the Rainbow, its present name stems from the fact that there was once a bush in the forecourt cut in the shape of a dove.

There is always a friendly welcome in this comfortable inn and during the winter you will find a roaring open fire. The real ales served are Bass, Friary Meux and Ansells Mild, with Olde English cider for those who prefer it. The wine list contains an unusually fine selection of Australian, American and European labels. As for food, you can choose a bar snack or opt for a full meal, for example cashew nut paella, mushroom balti, goujons of plaice and chicken or beef curry. Desserts include lemon meringue pie and spotted dick. A blackboard tells of daily specials. Outdoors is a large garden area where you can eat, if the weather is right, and in summer a barbecue is a popular feature there. The opening hours are from 11.30 am to 3 pm and 5.30 pm to 11 pm on Monday to Saturday and from 12 noon to 4 pm and 7 pm to 10.30 pm on Sunday.

Telephone: 01279 415419.

How to get there: If travelling on the M11, exit at junction 7 towards Chelmsford. Immediately turn left, signposted to Hastingwood, and the pub is 750 yards along on the left. Approaching from the east, follow the A414 from Ongar and Tylers Green and turn right before arriving at the large roundabout at the motorway access.

Parking: Park at the pub but please ask the landlord or bar staff for permission to leave your car while you walk.

Length of the walk: 4¼ miles. Map: OS Landranger 167 Chelmsford and Harlow (inn GR 482074).

Close though it is to the Hertfordshire border and just a short spin down the M11 to London, this area succeeds in showing you a typical pub and a true walk in the Essex countryside, with wide views to the south and east.

The Walk

Walk out of the pub exit onto the road and turn left for 80 yards to a concrete public footpath sign. Turn left here and go down a path, with a hedge on your left. At the field corner turn right, with a stream on your left. Carry on past a facing hedge, ignoring a stile on the right. Cross two plank bridges and go through a small, uncultivated section. Pass a thatched cottage on your left and join a track leading to a road and a concrete public footpath sign.

Turn right down this minor road, coming to the picturesque Shonks Cottage with the stream running by. Turn left along

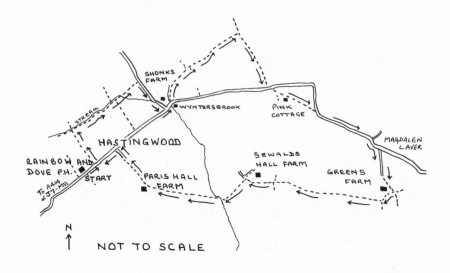

N

NOT TO SCALE

the road at a T-junction and immediately left up a broad green
lane. Look out for pigeon lofts on the right – a sight not so
often seen in the South! Continue up this wide grass track to a
T-junction of tracks 600 yards on. Turn right down a hedged
lane, which leads to a road at a public byway sign.

Cross straight over, marked with a public bridleway sign,
continuing until you reach a pink cottage and then the road
again. Walk along the road for 600 yards then turn right at a
sign which says 'Greens Farm', 'Magdalen Laver' and 'The
Chase'. Continue to a public byway sign and bear to the left of
the farm buildings. Just after two metal gates turn right
through the farm steading. At the end turn left down a track
for barely 50 yards, and opposite the back garden of the
farmhouse turn right along a reinstated path across a large
field. The line of the path crosses through a narrow thicket. At
the other side go over an uncultivated field.

Aim for a charred treestump in front of the farmhouse
ahead, Sewalds Hall Farm. At the end of this field identify a
rather basic stile with a yellow arrow pointing onwards. Cross
the gate of the stile and head uphill to the left of the farm

buildings, where a more civilised stile in a facing hedge allows you to pass by the rear of the farm up a lane for a few yards. A waymark points to the left. Follow this downhill across the field to a bridge over the Shonks Brook. Ahead you will see the buildings of Paris Hall Farm. Set off towards the section to the right of the house. The path passes through a gap in the buildings and then turns right on the farm drive for 450 yards to the road. Just before reaching the road you will see a little church that has been converted into a residential property.

Turn left along the road for 400 yards to return to the Rainbow and Dove.

Places of interest nearby

There are *pleasure boat trips* on the river Stort and navigation from Harlow Mill at nearby Harlow, just the other side of the M11 motorway – telephone 01992 767140. In Harlow itself is the *Mark Hall Cycle Museum*, which is open all year and offers a complete history of the evolution of the bicycle from the 'hobby horse' of the early 1800s to the super-light racing machines of the Tour de France in the 1990s. Telephone 01279 439680 for further information.

② Chipping Ongar
The Cock Tavern

Chipping Ongar has the air of a country market town, not surprisingly, since 'chipping' means market, and remains somehow aloof from the traffic passing through. It has considerable character and is a centre for the exploration of much charming country, while making no attempt whatever to capitalize on these potential assets. The High Street is pleasantly irregular, but the corner of the lane leading to the church strikes the most memorable note. This was at the heart of the community centuries ago. Beyond the church stood the castle, where a defensive position had been established before the Norman Conquest. Only the earthworks remain, the other side of an 18th-century house at the end of a private drive. The church itself, however, is humble, given that the town had some status even before 1066. Ongar is justly proud of its connection with Dr Livingstone of Stanley and Livingstone fame. He lived in a little room off the main street, serving his probation with the minister here, before he set out for Africa. What will happen to Ongar now that the railway link with Epping has gone, one wonders? Some say that it will die, but I have a fancy that this historic little town will rally.

The Cock is an interesting hostelry set in front of the castle mound and has a long history, dating back to 1580 in the time of the first Queen Elizabeth. It is a town pub, without a car park or garden but with white, timbered walls and a charm all of its own. Owned by Gray & Sons, it has, since the closure of the brewery, served Greene King IPA and Abbot Ale, with Shepherd Neame Master Brew Bitter frequently available. If it's cider you want, then Strongbow is the one on tap here. The Cock is well worth a visit, too, for the delights of its pub grub – nothing very daring but jolly good value for money. You will find various ploughman's lunches, shepherd's pie, jacket potatoes with different fillings and home-made soup. Of course, there are also freshly cut sandwiches, toasted if you wish. The opening hours are from 11 am to 3 pm and 6 pm to 11 pm on Monday to Saturday and from 12 noon to 3 pm and 7 pm to 10.30 pm on Sunday.

How to get there: Ongar lies just off the A414 between Chelmsford and Harlow. If travelling on the A12, take the A128 running north from Brentwood. The Cock is in the centre of the town, opposite the Budworth Hall.

Parking: There is no car park at the Cock but parking is possible close by on both sides of the High Street, at fairly modest charges (to help you with your calculations, the walk should take a little less than two hours).

Length of the walk: 3 miles. Map: OS Landranger 167 Chelmsford and Harlow (inn GR 552036).

Ongar is the centre of a comprehensive network of paths, in fact I used to think of it as the footpath capital of West Essex. Yes, many are the walks, both short and long, that can start

15

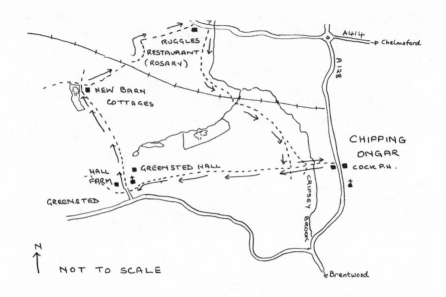

and finish in this pretty little town. This particular stroll passes by a fascinating, world famous place – the oldest wooden church in England, maybe in the whole of Europe. I do not hesitate to sing the praises of this route. Do try it for yourself.

The Walk

From the Cock cross the road, probably by the pedestrian crossing, and go down Bansons Lane at the side of the Budworth Hall. You will soon come to a pedestrian bridge over the Cripsey Brook. Continue up between the crops and pass through a hedge which faces you. The prospect is of a defined path in the field for ½ mile, with views of Chipping Ongar, back to your right. Very fine, you may think, and so it is. Before the advent of Dutch Elm disease this path was a magnificent 50 yard wide avenue with ancient elms on both sides, evidently there for horses and carriages to reach Greensted Hall ahead.

Cross the drive to the hall and pass over a stile. Continue, with a hedge on your right, to a kissing-gate which leads you to a little road by the church. This is a shrine of universal pilgrimage, unique in its sylvan setting, a wooden church with Saxon timbers built into its walls. Even if these were not so captivating for their age (1013), this primitive place of worship would draw people to it. Here are the oldest wooden walls in England. The trees felled to build this church were growing when the Romans came. So pause awhile in this historic setting – and as much for the beauty of the atmosphere as its history.

Continue the walk downhill past the church, through the buildings of Hall Farm. Follow this path, with the hedge on your right, climbing now to the hilltop. Turn slightly to the left and then turn right through some bushes to a track in the woods. Now turn right by New Barns Cottages. The path crosses a railway line on a substantial bridge. This was the continuation of the Central underground line from Epping to Ongar. Many were the threats to close this section and finally, just a few years ago, this was done.

From the bridge the track meanders downhill to Ruggles restaurant, marked as the Rosary on the OS Pathfinder map (1121). In the 1970s it was known as the Rose Tearoom, which then became the more ambitious business it now is. From the restaurant turn right along the pavement for a few yards. Just before a bridge turn right at a waymark to walk along the right bank of the Cripsey Brook. The river bends to the left and then you make for a tunnel arch under the railway line.

Through the tunnel, turn left to negotiate a thicket and emerge in a small field. The path continues, with the hedge on your right, all the way to the crossing of the path you originally took to the church. Turn left over the river bridge and walk up past the Budworth Hall, then cross back over the road to return to the Cock.

3 Great Easton
The Swan

Great Easton village is lovely, with some very pretty houses clustered around a small triangular green. Timbered and pargeted properties are well in evidence. The settlement grew up around a Norman castle, of which the round motte stands conspicuously beside the road in the grounds of the hall. There is good unconscious planning and a rare harmony in the alignment of this village. The church stands centrally, scenically on a little island, with the road flowing around it on one side and the churchyard path on the other. The curving road below is lined with dwellings of many periods, several of them very noteworthy.

The pub is situated about halfway down the main village street, a 500 year old building with nice bay windows. You will receive a grand welcome here, so when you have done this walk on the first visit, try another on the second or perhaps bring your friends to just sample the food, drink and ambience. The real ales are two of the best – Greene King IPA and Old Speckled Hen. Cider lovers can have Strongbow. There are two bars, public and saloon, wonderful old fashioned descriptions. The same goodies are on offer in both bars but in the saloon, which itself is a step into the past, there is a large open fireplace with appropriate accoutrements, such as a large saucepan. Food is available each lunchtime and evening and includes prawn and pineapple brochettes, crispy vegetables en croûte, chicken goujons and curries with naan bread and mushroom butter. Children are welcomed here in the secluded garden at the rear or in the Cygnet Room. The opening hours are from 11 am to 3 pm and 6 pm to 11 pm on Monday to Saturday and 12 noon to 3 pm and 7 pm to 10.30 pm on Sunday.

Telephone: 01371 870359.

How to get there: The B184 runs between Great Dunmow and Thaxted. Great Easton is well signposted off to the west of this road and the Swan is about 400 yards down the main village street on the right.

Parking: There is a good car park at the rear of the pub, but do ask permission if you want to leave your car there while you walk.

Length of the walk: 3 miles. Map: OS Landranger 167 Chelmsford and Harlow (inn GR 605255).

This is a splendid little walk. It is truly a feast to, in such a short time, have spectacular views and visit the gloriously diverse places of Great Easton, Duton Hill and tiny Tilty, with its abbey remains.

The Walk
From the Swan turn left up the hill. In a few yards come to the church with its very large churchyard. Norman builders constructed the nave and the vestry is built round a doorway

19

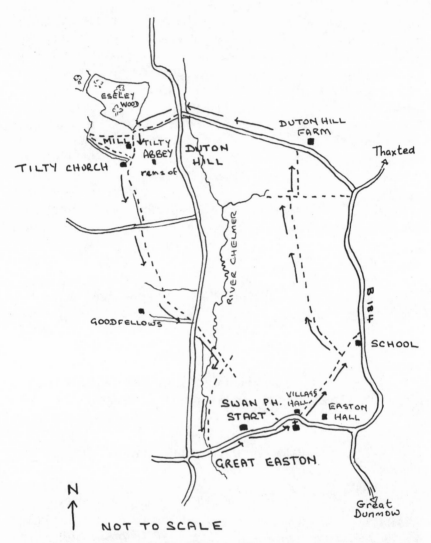

ESELEY WOOD

MILL

TILTY ABBEY

TILTY CHURCH

rems of

DUTON HILL

DUTON HILL FARM

Thaxted

RIVER CHELMER

GOODFELLOWS

B 184

SCHOOL

SWAN P.H. START

VILLAGE HALL

EASTON HALL

GREAT EASTON

Great Dunmow

N

NOT TO SCALE

of the same period. Just to the right of the village hall, by a concrete public footpath sign, go through a kissing-gate and continue onwards, north-east. To your right is Easton Hall, which has Tudor chimneys and a wing with 15th-century timbers.

The path you are on continues to a hedge and you

encounter two kissing-gates. About 100 yards from the end of this path, turn left on a distinct green track which runs along high ground, with splendid views of the Chelmer valley to your left and also onwards to the village of Duton Hill ½ mile ahead. Walk down to a stream, with a ditch on your right, and cross a bridge. Turn right and soon left uphill, with a hedge on the right, to a road at Duton Hill Farm. Turn left and walk downhill through the village. One of the houses is called Windy Ridge and that's what it must be sometimes. You pass the Three Horseshoes, Abbey Cottage and, at the bottom of the hill, the Rising Sun.

Cross over the river Chelmer and meet another road. At a concrete footpath sign opposite take a little path, with a stream on your left. This stream actually provided the water for Tilty Abbey, which we are approaching, and drove a mill on the same site.

Tilty church.

At the end of the field turn left over the stream, towards an iron gate. Continue, with a hedge on the left. Just at the mill building turn uphill in a field which often has large numbers of sheep. Today there is so little here – barely half a dozen houses – that it is difficult to realise how important Tilty was in years gone by. The Cistercians were adept at finding good sites which fulfilled their need for solitude and gave protection from the vanities of the world. This bit of land which sloped down to the Chelmer was ideal and they established an abbey here in 1153. The prosperity of the wool trade followed but by the 16th century the community's affairs had diminished and it suffered the fate of many of the religious houses, being suppressed in 1536.

The remains of the abbey are on the left, but ahead and still in good repair is the chapel outside the gates, which was traditional for all Cistercian houses. Somehow it was not destroyed at the Dissolution and much later it became the parish church. This then is Tilty, a little place but a memorable one.

Walk past the church after passing through a kissing-gate and at the road follow a concrete footpath sign opposite. The path passes through a hedge, then bears left to a road.

Turn right along the road for a few yards and go left at another concrete footpath sign. A barely visible path, which is half-right from the road, leads to a bridge. Continue in that direction for about 50 yards to cross another bridge. Now turn right along a broad green track to the road at the bottom of Great Easton. Turn left, uphill, for 200 yards to get back to the Swan.

4 Thaxted
The Swan Hotel

Thaxted is one of the principal tourist attractions among the little towns of Essex. The reason is obvious. It has style. Thaxted church with its great length and its proud, splendid spire is one of the many churches in the county which appear to be far too large for the needs of the neighbourhood, but we must bear in mind that, begun about 1340, it was constructed during the golden age of the Cutlers' Guild. This building is the glory of Thaxted, of Essex, of eastern England, and no man can praise it with adequate eloquence. Just as potent a symbol of Thaxted, however, is the 16th-century Guildhall, dominating the wide market street. Close by are many 15th-century neighbours. On the way to Broxted and not far from our route is the great Tudor Horham Hall. The name of the town is connected with the word thatch and means the place of reeds, these being obtained from the nearby river Chelmer.

Now run by the Old English Pub Company, the Swan, like

so many medieval inns, faces the church. Parts of the building date back to Domesday but most is 17th century. By going round to the back we can easily see how the first craftsmen made it. The real ales on draught are Courage Directors, John Smith's, Greene King IPA and Abbot Ale, with regularly changing guest beers. The thirsty walker who favours cider will find Strongbow. The inn is also a hotel and there is a full à la carte menu to be had – steaks, fish and vegetarian food, among other dishes. The bar snacks are tempting and include steak and ale pie, steak and kidney pie, jacket potatoes and sandwiches. A Sunday roast has become a regular feature, as in so many pubs these days. There is a patio area outdoors for eating and drinking and children are welcome there. Youngsters are not permitted in the bar, but can usually join you in the restaurant. The opening hours are from 11 am to 11 pm on Monday to Saturday and from 12 noon to 10.30 pm on Sunday.

Telephone: 01371 830321.

How to get there: Thaxted lies on the B184 between Great Dunmow and Saffron Walden. Approaching from the A120, this road passes Great Easton and is soon within the spell and sight of Thaxted church. Past the Guildhall, the Swan Hotel is opposite the church and you turn right to enter its car park.

Parking: Park at the Swan but please ask before leaving your car while you walk. There is a reception desk open from 7.30 am. I, of course, am not one of those who believes that before that time there is the ghost of an old man sitting on a chair to receive you – but locals say that he may sometimes be seen in the bar in the late evening . . .

Length of the walk: 3½ miles. Map: OS Landranger 167 Chelmsford and Harlow (inn GR 611310).

This is a gentle, rural walk with super views of the Chelmer valley, only a few miles from the river's source at Debden. Oh

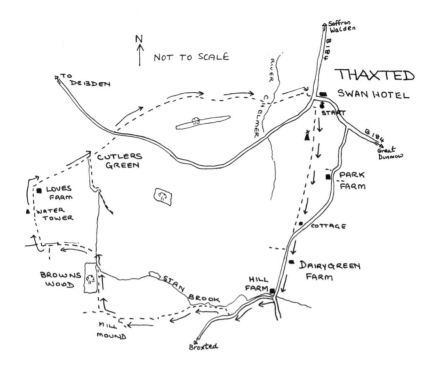

to be in Thaxted now that spring and summer are here, not to mention autumn and winter!

The Walk

Emerging from the Swan, cross the road to the church. To explore inside comes later – first we should do the walk and thus appreciate more the scope of the town. To the right of the church pass a concrete public footpath sign. Here is a charming scene, with the windmill framed between the two arms of a double row of almshouses. We walk between these two arms and go through a gate, passing closely another row of houses, to come to the windmill.

Immediately we are on a ridge, with views all around of great beauty. Continue to walk southward, soon descending to the back of a delightful cottage. The path passes round the

25

cottage to a road. Turn right here and ignore a concrete public footpath sign on your right. Pass Dairygreen Farm and Hill Farm, keeping right at a fork. The next bit is slightly tricky. There is at present no footpath sign, but after less than 400 yards from the road junction turn right up the bank and cross over the field to the side of the Stan Brook. Turn left and walk by the water for 130 yards. Now turn left, walking due west to the end of a projecting hedge. Pass this to a hedge corner 250 yards on.

The route continues along a field edge, with a hedge on your right, towards Mill Mound. Keep to the right of this through a woodland patch to a track. Turn right and go round a small mountain of sand to another track, this one slightly wider. Turn right along this, passing a wood on your left. Just beyond the trees the track swings to the left. At this point we are on the site of the railway branch line from Elsenham, which in fact terminated at a halt for Thaxted to the south-west of the town.

When you come to a junction of paths, turn right up a wide track towards a water tower. Pass Loves Farm and turn right through Cutlers Green. Thaxted's original prosperity was founded on the cutlery trade, which flourished for 200 years, probably to the extent that this spot was an overflow of the town in the industry's heyday. Whatever its origin, Cutlers Green is always a lovely place to walk through, with spaced out houses, some old, some new, set back from the lane.

Soon you will come to the Debden road. Cross with care to a public footpath sign and continue along a well-defined track. Before you is the glorious sight of Thaxted, laid out on a hill just under a mile ahead. Keeping this sight always in prospect, follow the path downhill and cross the young river Chelmer. With 400 yards to go, there is a steep climb up to the town, finally passing farm buildings to emerge onto a road at a concrete public footpath sign. Turn right to soon come to the church and the Swan Hotel across the road.

5 Little Burstead
The Duke's Head

Little Burstead is situated in beautiful countryside amid some of the prettiest hills in Essex. To the south of the village, built on a ridge, is the tiny 700 year old church. Its roof and font are 15th century and on the doorway are Mass dials by which the villagers told the time in the days before clocks. Two Elizabethan houses, Hatches Farm and Stockwell Hall, are encountered on the walk. The hall has a great timepiece with a face on which the figures are in blackened bones.

The Duke's Head is owned by Bass and serves, for example, Hancock's bitter, alongside Crouch Vale IPA from South Woodham Ferrers, with Dry Blackthorn cider on tap. The pub building is quite distinctive, though probably not older than 100 or so years. A good conservatory has been added along the front, which enhances the bar. To the side and rear is a splendid, extensive garden and if the weather is fine children are encouraged to make use of it. The menu is

A glimpse of Little Burstead House.

varied and includes 'Doorstep' sandwiches, gooey chocolate cake and, one of my favourites, salmon steak. The opening hours are 12 noon to 3 pm and 6 pm to 11 pm on Monday to Friday, 11 am to 11 pm on Saturday and 12 noon to 10.30 pm on Sunday.

Telephone: 01277 651333.

How to get there: If approaching from the A128, take the Billericay road at Herongate. Turn right at the T-junction, signposted to Little Burstead, and at the village centre turn left to the Duke's Head. From Billericay leave southwards on the B1007, soon turning right past Laindon Common to reach the pub.

Parking: Parking is plentiful in the area. If you want to leave your car at the pub while you walk, please ask permission at the bar.

Length of the walk: 3¾ miles. Map: OS Landranger 178 The Thames Estuary (inn GR 672928).

This walk explores a very attractive area. I do hope that you will return to repeat it at different seasons of the year and perhaps discover even more of the footpaths around Little Burstead.

The Walk

From the pub turn to the back of the building and head across the edge of a sports ground to a shed. Take the path to the right, with a thicket on your left. Now come to a stile bearing the immortal words 'bull loose in field'. To my knowledge there has been no such thing for many years, but each time I pass here I can't resist the temptation to look round the field!

Continue, with the fence on the left, over two stiles. Ignore a stile on your left but turn right downhill to cross a stile and steps into a wood. Pass a footpath sign for path 187 to enter an old estate. When you come to a T-junction take the right fork to a road. Turn left, passing the village pond by Hope Cottage.

At Little Burstead House, turn right across the road to a sign marked 'FP 52 Dunton'. Over a stile, walk with the hedge on the right. Continue over the open field to the corner, taking stock of the glorious views all around. Follow the hedge downhill to the left and cross a bridge, then turn right and soon turn left along a farm track, which soon turns right over a ditch. Follow this track to reach a stile on your left. Cross an uncultivated small field to another stile. Now cross this open field, aiming to the left of farm buildings almost 1 mile ahead. On your way you should find a stile taking you into a pasture field. Carry on with this line to a gap in the hedge into a green lane. Turn right uphill to the road at Botney Hill Farm.

Turn right on the road and walk downhill for ⅓ mile to a footpath sign on your left. Take this path uphill through a small piece of woodland, passing Hatches Farm. Cross the road to byway 45. Just past a white house, ignore a gate on

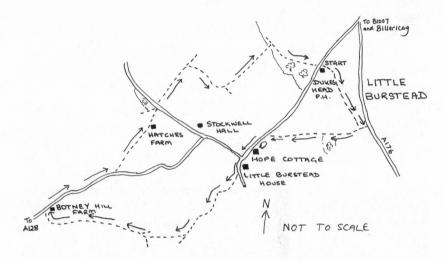

the right but turn right through a kissing-gate into a golf course. Follow the hedge and ditch on the right to a broad path. Turn left, with the Crouch on the right. The swampy area at the back of Stockwell Hall is said to be the source of the river. After 250 yards cross the bridge over the river and turn left with the hedge now on the left to the end of the course. Cross a kissing-gate and follow the path to the right, which leads you back to the Duke's Head.

⑥ Felsted
The Chequers

The Chequers stands in the centre of the village in front of the famous public school. It is a Ridleys house and the brewery is at nearby Hartford End. Presently run by a mother and daughter team, the atmosphere is extremely friendly both for locals, including schoolmasters, and visitors, including walkers. The real ales to consume are Ridleys IPA and the various seasonal beers which are a feature of the brewery's range. Strongbow cider is available on tap for those who prefer to 'quaff the apple brew'. The accommodation in the pub is surprisingly spacious, there being a public bar, a saloon, a restaurant, a children's room and another room, which amongst other uses can contain parties of ramblers sheltering from inclement weather. Plain food is the order of the day, but excellently prepared. Examples are vegetable soup, lasagne and a jacket potato, plaice with prawn and mushroom sauce, steak and kidney pie and, wait for it,

31

spotted dick! There is a small garden area at the rear of the building, which is adjacent to the school wall and provides a direct and close view of the school buildings. I wonder if this access has been used by present and past teachers and pupils! The opening hours from April to September are 11 am to 11 pm on Monday to Saturday and 12 noon to 10.30 pm on Sunday. In the winter the hours are 11 am to 11 pm on Friday and Saturday and 12 noon to 10.30 pm on Sunday, with the restricted hours of 11 am to 2.30 pm and 6 pm to 11 pm from Monday to Thursday.

Telephone: 01371 820226.

How to get there: Travelling north from Chelmsford on the A130, the road to Felsted is well signposted on the right, north of Howe Street. On the A120 east from Great Dunmow or west from Braintree take the turn offs clearly signposted to Felsted. The Chequers is in the middle of the village on the north side of the main street.

Parking: Parking is available in front of the pub and along the street. Please ask at the bar if you wish to leave your car at the pub while going on the walk.

Length of the walk: 4½ miles. Map: OS Landranger 167 Chelmsford and Harlow (inn GR 678204).

This is a very interesting short walk, taking in part of the disused railway line from Braintree to Bishop's Stortford, the redundant Felsted station and its present usage, a large bridge crossing the river Chelmer and the farm at Absol Park. The return takes you through Felsted Mill before climbing back to the village and all its attractive old buildings.

The Walk

On leaving the Chequers, turn right along the main street of the village. There is much to notice, including the preparatory school, the Boot restaurant, the Swan pub and, finally, the

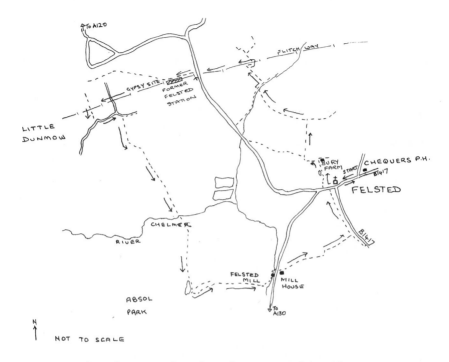

To A120

FLITCH WAY

GYPSY SITE
FORMER
FELSTED
STATION

LITTLE
DUNMOW

BURY
FARM
STABLES
CHEQUERS P.H.
B1417

FELSTED

CHELMER

RIVER

FELSTED
MILL
MILL
HOUSE

B1417

ABSOL
PARK

To
A130

N

NOT TO SCALE

Norman church. Past the church, turn right with a concrete public footpath sign. Continue to Bury Farm, bearing left past a large pond. Beyond the farmhouse, turn left along a waymarked track. At the first opportunity turn right with a yellow arrow, crossing a stile. The path follows a fence on your right. Also on your right are good views of the church and the school buildings.

At a crossing hedge turn left, with the hedge on your left, on a stony path. Cross a stile and the next small field to go over a bridge. Now turn right, soon passing a hedge, to turn left up the other side of this hedge. On reaching a high hedge, turn right for a few yards, then going back along the disused railway track. This has been developed by Essex County Council as the Flitch Way, a linear country park from Braintree to Bishop's Stortford, and can be a cool few minutes on a hot summer's day. At a road the bridge is no longer and steps lead down on the left.

Turn right along the road and left up some steps by a concrete public footpath sign. Here was Felsted station. Bear right by a Flitch Way sign. Much of the station area has been developed as a county gypsy site. Follow the arrows along your path and cross a bridge, then go up steps to regain the railway track. When you come to a sign pointing to Little Dunmow, turn left between two houses to a lane. Here turn left. Bear right at the T-junction and then turn right at a black public footpath sign to walk along a field edge, with a hedge on your right. Cross over an earth bridge and turn left along the hedge. When the hedge bears left, cross the field to the south-east, aiming for an oak tree. Now continue to the second telegraph pole and follow the waymark through a rough, uncultivated field to cross a large bridge over the river Chelmer. Look uphill (south-east) to a solitary post in a gap in the hedge. Walk uphill to this post, which leads to a farm track proceeding in a similar direction. Follow this track past a large pond.

Before you reach the farm buildings at Absol Park turn left, with a hedge on your left, and walk downhill over two fields. Cross a stile at the bottom of the hill and turn left in this paddock to go through two metal gates. Bear right over the bridge at the mill and follow the way through the mill grounds out to the road. Turn left and soon right by a concrete public footpath sign. Follow this well-used path uphill. Continue in this direction and at a crossing track turn left and soon right. At a crossing hedge, turn left along this fine old hedge, continuing for 100 yards to the road in Felsted, opposite the church. Turn right, back to the Chequers.

Langdon Hills
The Crown

It is said that there is nothing higher than Langdon in a line due north from here to the North Pole. At a height of 387 ft the hills at Langdon just beat Danbury although they are 100 ft lower than those in the north-west of the county. Of course, both Danbury and Langdon impress because they overlook the levels of great estuaries. The views all round this area are wonderful – pleasant woods, sloping meadows and waving crops lying immediately below. Almost at the top is the lofty tower of the new church, with its magnificent bells. The old church, now redundant but Tudor with some fittings of the Stuart period, is down the lane in a charming place not many yards from Goldfinches, passed on the walk. As the Basildon new town expanded it occupied the lower slopes of the hills, but several tracts of these upland woods have been preserved and provide delightful short walks.

At the peak of Langdon Hills is the aptly named Crown pub

and the present building has been in position since 1856. There are extensive facilities for families to eat and drink together, including a special room – but in fact children are welcome anywhere. The real ales are Burton Ale, Tetley Bitter and a guest beer which changes each month, and the cider is Addlestones Cask Conditioned. The food is traditional pub fare, with many popular items, such as scampi, steaks, pizzas, fish, baguettes and jacket potatoes with various fillings. The opening hours are 11 am to 11 pm on Monday to Saturday and 12 noon to 10.30 pm on Sunday. Dogs are not allowed inside but may join you in the large garden.

Telephone: 01268 414233.

How to get there: From the A13 take the exit signposted to Horndon on the Hill, the B1007. Follow the signs to Basildon to reach the Crown at the top of the hill. If coming from the north, join the A176 towards Basildon, passing Gloucester Park. At the large double roundabout join the B1007, which leads up to the pub.

Parking: Park at the pub, but please ask permission to leave your car there while going on the walk.

Length of the walk: 3½ miles. Map: OS Landranger 178 The Thames Estuary (inn GR 681867).

This is a marvellous area for short walks and this circuit is certainly no exception. If, like me, you fall in love with the district do come again and try some of the many other fine walks, perhaps to One Tree Hill and Horndon on the Hill.

The Walk

From the pub cross the B1007 with care and walk to your left, to and behind the cricket pavilion. You will often see a match in progress here. To continue the walk, go along the side of the wood behind the pavilion to reach a post where you enter the trees on a visible path. Continue downhill to reach a stile.

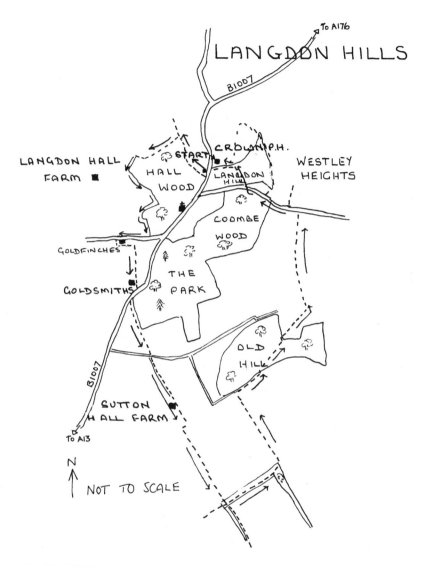

Don't cross this but turn left inside the wood along the bottom edge. Follow the yellow arrow and soon turn left, going uphill. After a few minutes turn right off the main path, keeping within sight of the edge of the wood. At each of three T-junctions turn right and you will get to a road beside a gate.

Turn right down this narrow lane, passing a house, Goldfinches. Turn left by a signpost marked 'FP 197 to Stanford le Hope' and at the end of the property turn left. Soon cross three stiles and turn right, with a fence on your right. Continue uphill to reach the main road by Goldsmiths.

Cross this road with great care and turn right downhill, passing an entrance to Langdon Hills Country Park. Soon you come to a footpath sign and you turn left with it over a stile. Some attempt has been made to make this path double hedged but part of it is overgrown and it may be easier to walk on the field. Cross a stile by a footpath sign onto a little lane. Go straight over and continue on FP 32 down a green lane to Sutton Hall. Cross a stile and walk on through a double hedged track.

At the corner of the field turn right for a few yards to turn left over a stile. Here walk over an open field, through a gap in the hedge, and continue on to enter a narrow wood over a plank bridge. Watch out! This can be slippy at times. Inside the wood there is a four-way footpath sign. Ours is to the left, marked 'One Tree Hill'. Follow the well-walked path, keeping to the southern part of the wood. On reaching the end of the wood, turn left to another multi-footpath sign. You should follow the 'Old Hill' direction across the open field to a footpath sign in the hedge opposite.

Cross through the hedge and turn right for a few yards up a track, and on reaching two gates to private properties turn left through a narrow gap. This leads to a forest track. There is a newly constructed bridleway on your left but follow the old pathway to the north-east until you reach a broad crossing track. Turn left up this for a few yards, looking out for a stile on the right. Walk down and cross this, continuing your original direction by a waymark and stile and onwards.

Behind a large shed you will see another waymark and stile. Cross this, turning right to another stile. Having crossed, turn left along an old track leading through a gate to Northlands Farm. It may be easier to use the gate to the left and follow the farm road back to the right, leading out to the road.

Turn left along this sometimes busy thoroughfare, ignoring the first footpath sign on the right. Just after a bend, to the right, a sign marked 'Westley Heights FP 174' is ours. Go through the gate and bear left. Bear left at two left forks and on reaching the side road to the Westley Heights car park turn left to the Crown.

Places of interest nearby
Due east of the pub but south of Basildon itself, is *Basildon Zoo*, at London Road, Vange. The zoo is open throughout the year and features a small collection of birds and animals including some endangered species. Telephone 01268 553985. Also within easy reach of the pub and affording good views of the busy river Thames, is *Tilbury Fort*. It is an English Heritage property and is open all year. Telephone 01375 858489.

Boreham
8 The Queen's Head

Boreham, which is in close proximity to Chelmsford, is one of the most interesting villages in the area, with a fascinating church and one of the finest Tudor halls in Essex. New Hall is to be found tucked away to the north-west of the village and is a palace built by Henry VIII on land seized from Ann Boleyn's father after she had been beheaded on Tower Hill. It stands nearly 90 yards wide with projecting wings and six bays. Henry celebrated the feast of St George and Merrie England here and, later, Queen Elizabeth paid a five day visit. Converted into a home for French refugees in the 18th century, it is now a convent.

The Queen's Head is a splendid example of a village pub. Nestling beside the church, the building dates back to the 16th century and still has two rooms designated in the old style, as a public bar and a saloon. There is also a secluded garden and an outside drinking area. Good pub food is available from

12 noon to 2.15 pm every day and from 6 pm to 9 pm on Monday to Saturday. Wednesday and Sunday lunchtimes are 'roast days'. On other days special dishes are offered on the blackboard and a popular choice is always 'Breakfast in bread' – French bread filled with sausage, tomato, bacon and mushrooms. There are vegetarian options and examples of other dishes are scampi, plaice and the 'Big Fry-up' of sausages, bacon, egg, baked beans and fried bread. This is one of the many Gray's houses that are spread over this part of Essex and the real ales are Greene King IPA and Abbot, from handpumps. Children of 14 and over are welcome with their parents, or younger if eating. The actual opening hours at the pub are 10.30 am to 3 pm and 5 pm to 11 pm on Monday to Saturday, 12 noon to 3 pm and 7 pm to 10.30 pm on Sunday.

Telephone: 01245 467298.

An ancient house at Boreham.

How to get there: From the A12, either at Springfield or Hatfield Peverel, take the B1137 and follow the signs to Boreham. Approaching from the east, turn down Plantation Road by the Six Bells pub and at the T-junction go right for a few yards. The Queen's Head is on the right, just before the church. From the west, turn right opposite a wine merchants' and the pub is beside the church.

Parking: Space is limited at the pub, but there is free parking in the street outside.

Length of the walk: 3¾ miles. Map: OS Landranger 167 Chelmsford and Harlow (inn GR 756096).

This walk is full of interest, with an outward route above the valley bottom followed by a return along the river itself. The village's historical royal connection is not obvious but is worth seeking out.

The Walk
Leave the pub and turn left along Church Road, passing some interesting old houses on your right. Turn right with the road and cross over to a public footpath sign pointing east along a wide track. This delightful route goes along a contour above the Chelmer valley for about a mile, passing Culverts Farm and Brakey Wood. Turn right with the track to Belstead Cottages and then left out to the road.

Turn right and follow the road round, crossing the Chelmer and Blackwater Navigation on Paper Mill Bridge. Immediately turn right through a gate and follow the bank for 1 mile. Just after crossing a metal bridge over the Sandon Brook, you arrive at a road.

Turn right on the road and cross the Chelmer, then go left on the towpath, following the canal for 400 yards almost to the Little Baddow Lock. Turn right towards Boreham church and follow the waymarks, bearing left at a wood and crossing right over a bridge to pass between two large houses. On

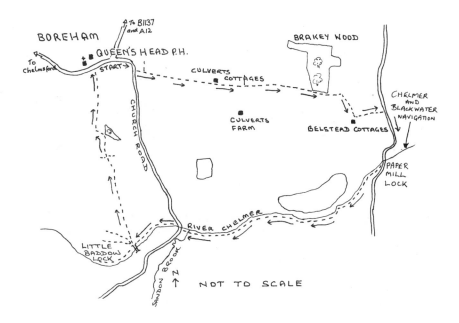

reaching a road you will observe that the church and pub are just to your left.

Take time to explore this intriguing village, if you can, and be sure to look inside the church. It is mainly 13th and 14th century, with a fine central tower standing much as the Normans left it. The arch facing the nave shows the Roman tiles mixed with stones which the Normans used and below that is a 14th-century addition. We come into the church through a porch with much medieval timber in its walls. It once carried on to the gate as a shelter for the congregation. The font is 14th century and has panels of painted flowers in vases. There is medieval craftsmanship in a screen of six bays in the tower and one with twelve heads in the aisle.

9 Terling
The Rayleigh Arms

The story of the beautiful village of Terling is much grander than its present simple appearance would imply. Many of the farmhouses have Tudor chimneys and throughout the parish there is a richness of overhanging gabled roofs. At one time Henry VIII had a palace here. Among many other notable people connected with the village was John William Strutt, the third Lord Rayleigh, who in Victorian times was regarded as one of the most learned men who ever lived in England. For nearly half a century he carried out his work of scientific discovery in Terling. He received wide recognition and was awarded the Nobel prize in 1904.

The Rayleigh family have occupied Terling Place for many centuries and in 1825 his lordship, needing a sort of overspill to accommodate his guests at the big house, constructed the building which was then partly an inn and is now the pub – hence its name. It is often called the Monkey, too, because of the family coat of arms on the pub sign which features, in part, a monkey. A freehouse, the regular beers here are

Adnams and Crouch Vale IPA, with a series of guest beers. A tap dispenses Strongbow cider and there are obviously fans of draught Guinness in the area. The opening hours are from 12 noon to 3 pm on Friday to Sunday and each evening from 6 pm to 11 pm (7 pm to 10.30 pm on Sunday). This is a pub that concentrates on its liquid refreshment, but you will certainly find bar snacks here at lunchtime on Friday and Saturday. If there is no food available on Sunday, please ask at the bar for permission to eat your own food on the premises. Telephone: 01245 233228.

How to get there: Terling can be easily reached from the A12 between Colchester and Chelmsford. Leave the A12 at Hatfield Peverel, where a road goes past the station and on to Terling. Turn left in the centre of the village and right at a T-junction. The pub is not hard to find.

Parking: In the pub car park. Please let the pub staff know if you want to leave your car there for the duration of the walk. There is also parking available opposite the village hall.

Length of the walk: 3¾ miles. Map: OS Landranger 168 Colchester and The Blackwater area (inn GR 771151).

Terling is probably one of the most attractive villages in Essex. The walk explores some of its best features, which are close to the village along the Ter valley, and returns on part of the Essex Way, over paths and little lanes.

The Walk
Leaving the pub, turn right and pass Owl Hills House. The streets in Terling have many interesting old dwellings. Turn left at the first opportunity to a ford over the river Ter. The road climbs past a little green at Bramley Cottages. At a fork turn right, signposted to Great Waltham. In a few yards you will see the windmill and if you wish you can turn down the lane to inspect it even more closely. Having done so, resume

The windmill at Terling.

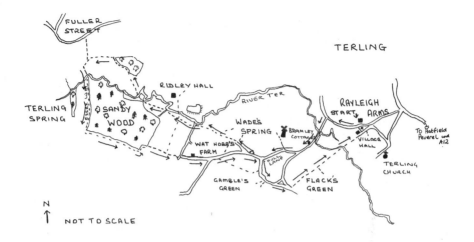

your original line up the little road, which will soon be identified as Hull Lane.

Continue to your right and bear right at a telephone kiosk by Oakfield Lane. At its end keep to the right of a hedge, walking along a field edge. There are fine views from here of the windmill and you can also see Terling and Fairstead churches. At the field corner do not turn left but continue in the same direction over the field. Presently, cross a stile and walk on, with a fence on your left. At the fence corner turn left to reach a gate by the river. At this point turn left and right through another gap, with the hedge on your right. Continue until you come to more gates, still fairly close to the river. After the last gate walk over a field to the far corner of a wood. Here there is sometimes an improvised gate which you should go through and reassemble. Walk straight across over a rather neglected meadow, to a bridge with two stiles. Uphill now to a grass track. Turn left along this, following the edge of a thicket round to go through two gaps into a field near Fuller Street. Turn left, with a hedge on your left.

At the field corner follow the Essex Way sign over a ditch and continue on a visible path round the corner of the next field. When the hedge ends turn left down to a bridge and cross a meadow. Pass through a gate and walk up the side of Sandy Wood. At the top follow the Essex Way arrow to the left. Now you go along the extent of the wood from west to east. At the corner keep to the edge of the wood until you reach an Essex Way post pointing across the field along a path left between the crops. On your left are good views of the Ter valley and, in particular, Ridley Hall.

Cross a stile and a meadow, then another stile into a little lane up to a duck pond. Walk on from here till you come to a phone box. Turn right at a point where Hull Lane turns left. Follow this road round to a second green, signposted to Boreham. You will come to a five-barred wooden gate with a small gate at its side. Pass through this and walk slightly uphill, with a hedge on your left. This pretty path passes a cricket pitch, a tennis court and a swimming pool. Next you come to the village hall. Immediately past this, turn left by a narrow path to reach a gate opposite the Rayleigh Arms.

10 South Benfleet
The Hoy and Helmet

The Hoy and Helmet is a splendid old pub, the first part of its name coming from the type of broad sailing boat used to transport the produce of local farmers. It is situated close to Benfleet Creek, which runs into Hadleigh Ray and then the Thames, the creek separating the village of South Benfleet from Canvey Island. The Danes set up a camp in the area in AD 893, but Alfred's men were too much for them and took off to London all the ships that they didn't burn. This was verified by the discovery of skeletons and timbers when the railway was constructed. The church, just behind the pub, dates back about 500 years and its perfect symmetry attracts artists and architects from far and wide. The oldest part is in the inner wall of the tower, where there is a Norman doorway between two stopped up windows. Inside is an amazing mass of carved wood crowded into a tiny space with no suggestion of confusion.

A well-marked entrance into the country park.

In the 19th century this pub was a smuggling centre and tunnels exist below the car park. The beers available here are Theakston Best Bitter, XB and Old Peculier. If it's cider you want, there's Strongbow. For further sustenance, choose from, for example, a steak sandwich, steak and kidney pie, Cumberland sausage, vegetable lasagne or, on Sundays, opt for a two course roast meal. Daily specials appear on a chalkboard. The opening hours are from 11 am to 11 pm on Monday to Saturday and 12 noon to 10.30 pm on Sunday.

Telephone: 01268 792307.

How to get there: From the A130 at the Sadlers Farm roundabout go east to Tarpots and, at a mini-roundabout, go south to reach Benfleet church and turn right for a few yards to the Hoy and Helmet. Approaching from the A13 and Southend, turn left on the B1014 and after a mile reach the pub.

Parking: The Hoy has a large car park, but please ask permission to leave your car there while walking.

Length of the walk: 4½ miles. Map: OS Landranger 178 The Thames Estuary (inn GR 778861).

In a highly populated area such as this, an amble on the Benfleet Downs is doubly refreshing. On a return visit why not try walking to Leigh and getting the train back.

The Walk

Leave the Hoy and Helmet and turn left up the hill. Pass the church and keep going east along the B1014. Up on the skyline to the left a large tower appears – it looks like a church but was in fact an ornate water tower. When you come to a left-hand bend turn right at a public footpath sign. After 100 yards cross two stiles and walk between a hedge and a fence. After another 100 yards cross a stile by a public footpath sign and bear left, with a hedge on your right. Cross a stile beside two footpath signs, then turn left (your original direction) and walk along the field edge, with a ditch on your left. At the field corner turn right.

Soon you see views over Benfleet Creek to Canvey Island and the Thames. Turn left down steps to a fenced path through woods. Turn right then pass brambles into the open area within the country park. Keep on, with a hedge on the left and fine views on the right. You come to a bench – a rest for some? Beyond the bench, soon turn right along a broad, grassy path leading down to a gravel track. Turn left and cross the stream. Continue uphill, then turn left through a kissing-gate to follow a fence on your right and reach another bench, this one dedicated to our old friend and colleague Bill Thatcher, a moving force in the foundation of the country park.

Pass through a gap and go on to another kissing-gate at the park boundary. Here you can choose steps or path. Later on turn right at a waymark, through a gate to a lane. Turn right

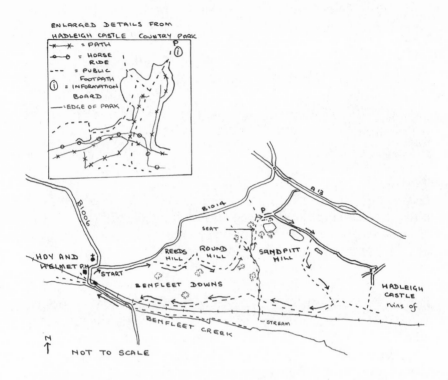

past a footpath sign, then cross a stile into an old road. Turn
right over a stile and look for a footpath sign to your right.
Continue to follow signs to your left to cross a stile. You will
see the castle ruins to your left. Come to a three-way footpath
sign. If you wish, you can walk to the castle by turning left.
The route we are following, however, is to the right. Do not
cross the kissing-gates at a footpath sign but keep right of the
hedge on the park path. Follow this to the west, staying north
of the railway line to the park extremity at School Lane. Here
make your way back to the Hoy and Helmet.

11 Woodham Ferrers
The Bell Inn

Woodham Ferrers is a pretty village which sits on top of little hills running down to the Crouch valley, its houses lining a winding street. In recent times a large town development has grown around Woodham Ferrers station, about 1½ miles to the south. The village has so far resisted the movement to amalgamate into the town and has asserted its right to the name Woodham Ferrers, whilst insisting that the town be called South Woodham Ferrers. It is associated with Woodham Walter and Woodham Mortimer some miles to the north. The story is that the local family in Norman times had three brothers, who each put a name to one of these three settlements. How proud they must be, if they are watching now, at the relatively unspoilt nature of their charges.

The Bell Inn is on the site of a brewery associated with the time of the building of the church 500 years ago. It became a Baddow Brewery pub in 1885 and is now a freehouse. From being very small it has been much enlarged over the intervening years. Its natural geographical advantages, like its position on the hill, with surrounding valleys, and the countryside atmosphere so close to a new town, make the Bell a popular place. The real ales are Adnams Bitter and Ridleys IPA, both excellent beers, the latter brewed not too far away, and Strongbow cider is on tap. There is a good selection of lunchtime food, such as trout, haddock, chicken tikka and seafood platter, as well as sandwiches and rolls. Nine varieties of fillings for jacket potatoes are on offer, and seven different soups. You can have fillet, sirloin, rump or T-bone steak, and on a Sunday you can opt for a roast meal. To follow, does your mouth water at the thought of sticky toffee meringue (coffee flavoured meringue with lots of cream) or even 'Louisiana Love Bite' (caramel ice-cream with nuts and chocolate)? The opening hours are from 11 am to 3 pm and 6 pm to 11 pm on Monday to Saturday and from 12 noon to 3 pm and 7 pm to 10.30 pm on Sunday.

Telephone: 01245 320443.

How to get there: At the Rettendon Turnpike roundabout, the junction of the A130 and the A132, follow the signs to South Woodham Ferrers. Turn left at the second roundabout, taking the B1418, and about ¾ mile north arrive at the Bell on the right.

Parking: There is a fairly large car park by the pub. Please ask at the bar if you intend leaving your car there while you walk.

Length of the walk: 3½ miles. Map: OS Landranger 167 Chelmsford and Harlow and 168 Colchester and The Blackwater area – the walk is partly on each (inn GR 798994, shown on the Chelmsford map).

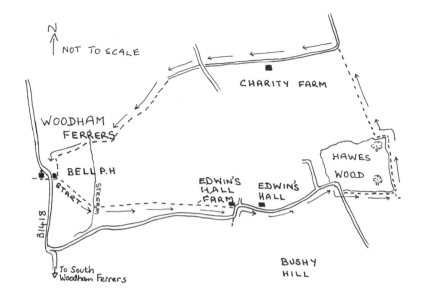

The paths around are certainly some of the finest in southern Essex, possessing as they do scenic beauty and great variety.

The Walk

The walk starts by leaving the pub premises from the rear of the garden. Follow a path to the south-east, half-right and downhill across a field. Go through a thicket and over a stile and stream. Continue with quite a stiff climb towards a hedge. Through a gap in the hedge aim for the right-hand edge of Edwin's Hall Farm. Go past the wooden fence on your left to cross a stile onto the road.

Turn left and follow the road, soon passing the impressive looking buildings which are Edwin's Hall. To your right at this point is Bushy Hill, at one time a key piece of Marconi's communications network. Continue, joining Hawes Wood on your left and turning right with the road to a concrete public footpath sign. The path continues with the wood on its left. At the end of the trees turn left up a wide bridleway. This used to

55

be a muddy monster but County Council work has made its passage on foot much more bearable. Follow the bridleway up to the end of the wood and turn left, then soon right along a green lane to reach the corner of a lane. Here we have reached a wide plateau of land which extends above the valley.

Turn left along the lane, passing Charity Farm. When you reach a crossroads, walk on, with a pond on your left, bearing left across a field to another pond. Follow the power lines, but at some yards distance, to reach a path going downhill, with a hedge on your left. At the bottom cross a stile and bear left to a gate. Having crossed this, go into the adjacent field and make for the backs of houses up above you. Turn left along the garden fences and return to the precise opening into the pub garden where the walk commenced.

Take time, if you can, to explore the church on your return. Standing with a good view of the Crouch valley below, it is a wide, open building of the 13th century and has lost its tower. Inside you will find a 14th-century font and four 15th-century benches. Over the high chancel arch a wall displays all that remains of a medieval doom painting, in which Christ sits on a rainbow. A delightful monument is a son's tribute to his mother, showing Cecilie Sandys, widow of the Archbishop of York, kneeling, in painted alabaster, a lady of Jacobean days, below a graceful trellis covered with flowers, Father Time with an hourglass in his hand lurking in the shadow of a column behind her.

Greenstead Green
12 The Hare and Hounds

Greenstead Green is not to be confused with the hamlet that has a similar name (though a slightly different spelling) west of Chipping Ongar. This one lies 1 mile south-east of Halstead and is an unspoiled place above the Bourne Brook, not a long way from its joining with the river Colne. I first visited this village almost 30 years ago en route for a party in Greenstead Hall. This sounds very grand and indeed the hall was at the time part of the estate of Lord Butler of Saffron Walden (the famous Rab). However, Rab had arranged for it to be used by staff and lecturers from the Essex University. To this day a footpath runs from Stanstead Hall through the grounds of Greenstead Hall to Halstead. As a result of the village lying so near the brook there are structured slopes on both sides and the high church tower can be seen from all around.

Despite the comparative smallness of Greenstead, until recently there were two pubs facing each other across the little green. Now the Plough has become a private residence and the debate as to which of the two was the favourite is at an end – the Hare and Hounds is the local without dispute. It lies in an acre of land with pleasant gardens to the rear, facing downhill towards the brook, and its building is neat, comprising two separate bars. The real ale purveyed is usually the ever popular Greene King IPA, but from time to time guest beers are stocked. Strongbow draught cider is offered in the spring and summer. Bar snacks, such as ploughman's lunches, are available, as well as hot food, for example scampi and, often, home-made steak and kidney pies. Children are welcome if eating with adults. In the spring and summer the hours are from 11.30 am to 3 pm and 7 pm to 11 pm on Monday to Saturday and 12 noon to 3 pm and 7 pm to 10.30 pm on Sunday. In the winter the Hare and Hounds is open every evening, but at lunchtime on Wednesday, Saturday and Sunday only.

Telephone: 01787 477996.

How to get there: Greenstead Green lies north of the A120 between Braintree and Colchester. Take the turning to Stisted and follow the signs north from this village to come to the Hare and Hounds after about 2½ miles.

Parking: This is no problem and you can leave your car outside the pub or on the road in such a quiet village.

Length of the walk: 3 miles. Map: OS Landranger 168 Colchester and The Blackwater area (inn GR 823278).

A picturesque walk down to the brook and along a meadow, then up to Nightingale Hall and over to the hamlet of Burton's Green, with views of Earls Colne and Greenstead Green church. You go through a quaint little farm before crossing the brook back to the pub.

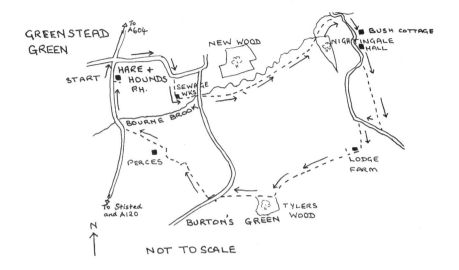

The Walk

Turn right from the pub and soon pass the village sign, then turn right again down a lane signposted to Burton's Green. At a sharp corner walk straight on down a track to a water treatment plant. Pass the plant, with a hedge on your right, to reach the Bourne Brook at the corner of the field. Turn left back to the road, then go right over a bridge to a black footpath sign on the left. Now turn left along a visible path over an uncultivated field. At the end cross a ditch and bear right to a gap in the facing hedge.

Through the gap, turn left and continue, with the hedge on your left. Walk past a small wood. Ignore a five-bar gate on your left and continue to a bridge at a black public footpath sign by Newhouse Road. Turn right up a steep hill past Bush Cottage and Nightingale Hall as far as a concrete public footpath sign. Through the hedge, bear right past a telegraph pole up a hill towards a gap in the facing hedge. In this gap is a rather ancient stile by a metal gate. Continue in the same line across the field to a stile by a metal gate and a concrete public footpath sign. Now turn right for 100 yards down the road to another footpath sign. Follow this, aiming towards the house at Lodge Farm.

Turn right along the farm track, past buildings on your right, then continue on a grass track between two fields. When you reach the end of the field cross a ditch by this track, aiming for a solitary tree ahead. Having reached this tree, locate a gap in the hedge in front of you. Through the gap, turn left to the field corner and then go right along the field edge to a lane by a black public footpath sign.

Walk to your left for a few yards, then turn right at a footpath sign and enter a field, with a house on your left. There is a fine view of Greenstead church. Follow the path down the side of the field and negotiate a tree trunk to go into a tiny wood. At its end cross a stile into a little field. This whole area is reminiscent of the countryside as it looked 60 years ago. Walk down the field to a gate and go through leftwards into a farm track. Now continue uphill past some farm buildings and on to a road. Follow the road over the Bourne Brook and bearing right uphill to the Hare and Hounds.

13 Hockley
The Bull

South of the Bull is the extensive woodland identified on the map as the Hockley Woods. However, part at least is known as the Great Bull Wood and on the far south-west is Bullwood Hall, which is now government property and in whose grounds has grown up a prison. Clearly the hall was named after the woods, but did they get their name from the pub, there having been an alehouse on the site since 1560, or was it the other way round? It is interesting to speculate. Hockley's houses are ranged on a hill between these woods and the valley of the Crouch. One can imagine the Saxons fleeing for safety into the depths of the trees before the vengeance of Canute's Danes, who on the slopes below had won for their leader the crown of England.

The Bull is a fine old-world pub where visitors are given a friendly welcome. These days the Country Pub Co owns the freehold, together with two more old inns. There are four real ales, Courage Directors, John Smith's and two guest beers which are changed frequently. Two ciders are stocked, Scrumpy Jack and Strongbow. The food is all home-cooked. As well as sandwiches and a variety of filled jacket potatoes, you can have steak and kidney or steak and mushroom pie, chilli and rice, gammon steak and daily specials. There are large gardens with attractions for children at the rear of the pub, set back from the road and backing onto the woods. This, of course, is a popular venue in summer. The opening hours are 11 am to 11 pm on Monday to Saturday and 12 noon to 10.30 pm on Sunday.

Telephone: 01702 203122.

How to get there: From the Basildon to Southend-on-Sea road, the A127, turn off at Rayleigh Weir and follow the signs to Hockley. The B1013 from Rayleigh High Street climbs up and after 2 miles or so passes the Bull on the right. Travelling south from Chelmsford on the A130, turn left at the traffic lights at Rawreth. Go right at the T-junction, then under a railway bridge to the B1013, where you turn left to the Bull.

Parking: Park at the pub car park, which is big, but please ask at the bar before leaving your car while you go for the walk. There is also a car park in the woods just behind the pub.

Length of the walk: 4 miles. Map: OS Landranger 178 The Thames Estuary (inn GR 833924).

This walk is in largely peaceful countryside, wonderfully unexpected in such a populated area. The most surprising feature, so relatively close to Southend-on-Sea, is the elevation of the paths, which on a clear day offer outstanding views.

The Walk

From the Bull cross the B1013, Hockley High Road, into Bull Lane by a concrete public footpath sign. Soon take the right

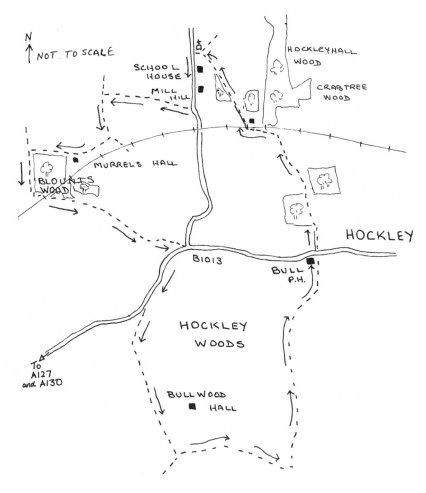

fork on an unmade track. Follow this between gardens out to an estate road, where you turn right and immediately left at a footpath sign. Continue on this path to the end of a sports field. Here the definitive path bears left to a clump of trees over the field. Most people, however, turn right and follow the field edge to the railway line, then turn left to the woods.

Follow the path through the woods. At the next field corner turn right over the railway by a bridge and come to a lane at a house called Hawthorns on St Peters Road. Follow the road

The Bull Inn

LARGE
BEER
GARDEN
And
BARBECUE
PARK

north to reach two footpath signs and take the left path, walking on to reach the church.

Take a look inside, if you have the time. No Saxon work is traceable today, for the oldest thing to be seen is the marble font, brought here about the time of Magna Carta, when most of the present church was built. The three round pillars between the nave and aisle have the conventional foliage of that time, but the nave roof is 14th century, with well-moulded capitals and kingposts. The curious looking tower was begun some 600 years ago, the lower stage being square and solid. Where the buttresses end it becomes octagonal, with battlements surrounding a small spire.

Turn left when you reach the road, passing School House and Mill Hill, and continue downhill. Before coming to a railway bridge turn right down Murrels Lane, walking on for 500 yards to a T-junction. Turn left and follow the lane. Just before Murrels Hall turn right on a wide grassy track. This continues into a large field, with the north edge of Blounts Wood on your left. At the end of the wood turn left over a plank bridge and walk just inside the trees. Nearing the railway line, which is elevated, look to your left for a path up to a white metal stile which leads to a level crossing over the line, then a further stile down to the field on the other side. The path runs east along the side of the woods, now on the outside, and climbs out of the valley. Bear right to a metal gate. At this point cross a stile and walk, with the hedge now on your right, onwards and upwards, finally on a path between gardens leading out to Hockley High Road. Turn right along this busy road, crossing with care.

Turn left down Bullwood Hall private road (despite all the 'private' notices this is most certainly a public footpath – see the black footpath sign). The reason for all the security is that Bullwood Hall is a prison. Just before the most exclusive sign of all a very old public footpath marker points you off the road to the right along a row of chestnut trees. Presently an extended view of Rayleigh presents itself on the right. You come to a yellow arrow pointing straight on, then turn left, almost immediately, along a crossing path towards the Great Bull Wood. Follow the path on the edge of the trees then continue inside them, still at the edge. At a crossroads of paths, with barriers to prevent the entry of horses, turn left, going north to a junction of bridleways. Here turn left and right, straight on, that is, and follow the bridleway waymarks all the way to Hockley Woods car park. Climb up to the car park, then turn left and in only a few yards you will reach the Bull.

⒕ Paglesham
The Punchbowl

To the north-east of Southend-on-Sea, part of Rochford District, including Canewdon and Paglesham, is enclosed by the rivers Roach and Crouch. Paglesham, though only a few miles away from the centre of Southend, is altogether in a different world and is made up of two tiny settlements – Paglesham Churchend and Paglesham Eastend. The church and its cottages, some of them all wood, stand in a row looking across the fields to the far horizon. Churchend, unlike Eastend, has no oysters but this group of buildings is as delightful as any in the county. The road ends beside the hall and church but before this we pass an exceedingly attractive row of cottages, brick and plaster with steep red roofs, and a surprisingly tall, weatherboarded inn which is the Punchbowl. Most of the church is Norman and it is a slightly smaller version of the one at nearby Canewdon. It is remarkable that all the doors have been opening and shutting, ever since the church was new, on the same strap-hinges. Yes, it is no surprise that Paglesham is a favourite haunt of many people and well worth a visit at any time of the year.

The real ales at the Punchbowl are Old Speckled Hen, Wadworth 6X, Adnams Bitter and often a guest beer, with Dry Blackthorn as the cider on tap. The food is varied and attractively priced. Steak and kidney pudding and hot dogs in a long roll are traditional favourites, while slightly less usual are Italian stew and Cajun chicken. There is a sizeable garden at the back and children are welcome here and in the restaurant. The opening hours are 11.45 am to 3 pm and 7 pm to 11 pm on Monday to Saturday and 12 noon to 3 pm and 7 pm to 10.30 pm on Sunday.

Telephone: 01702 258376.

How to get there: From Rochford and the B1013 follow the road east past Ballards Gore. Beyond Biggins Farm at a sharp right-hand bend go straight on to Churchend. From the A130 at Battlesbridge take the road past Hullbridge and Ashingdon, then turn left towards Paglesham, where indicated, to reach Ballards Gore.

Parking: Some parking is available at the pub but please ask at the bar before leaving your car.

Length of the walk: 5 miles. Map: OS Landranger 178 The Thames Estuary (inn GR 923932).

Much of this walk is along the sea wall, looking first towards Wallasea Island and then south-east towards Potton Island across the river Roach. It links both parts of Paglesham and will probably take you two and a half hours, although you may well wish to dally at Eastend. I hope you will try this circuit – a complete contrast to the inland routes in the book.

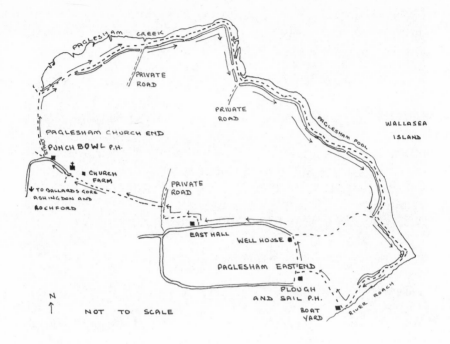

The Walk

A few yards west of the pub a black public footpath sign
stands beside a concrete one. Our route goes half-left, turning
gradually to the right, and goes alongside some young trees to
the sea wall. On the wall turn right, to the east, and follow it
beside Paglesham Creek. On your left is the western part of
Wallasea Island and only a mile or so away on the far bank of
the river Crouch is Burnham-on-Crouch.

After about 2 miles the path on the wall turns sharp right
and continues, with Paglesham Pool to your left. Follow the
wall for a further 1½ miles and walk on to the boat-building
yard at Paglesham Eastend. Turn right off the wall on a public
footpath behind the Plough and Sail public house. Here turn
right along a track through the garden of Well House to a lane
in front of the house. Turn left along this lane, walking west
for ½ mile to East Hall Farm.

Immediately before reaching the farm turn right at a

Paglesham church.

concrete footpath sign. Behind the farm buildings another concrete sign points left (westwards) towards a farm track. Although, according to the map, the path runs diagonally across the field to a five-barred gate, it appears that the local route follows the track around a corner to the same gate. Over to your right a large windpump is in operation. At the gate turn left at a concrete footpath sign (this is embedded in brambles and may be impossible to see in the summer).

Follow a nice field edge path for ½ mile, finally passing through a large garden between the church and a house (named Winton). On your left a very large pond appears as you reach the road at Churchend. Now a short stroll by a farm and several cottages brings you back to your starting point at the Punchbowl.

15 Tolleshunt D'Arcy
The Queen's Head

This pub sits in the square in the middle of this charming old village, which at one time boasted three butchers and three bakers. There are still three pubs within the village, which may tell us something about our modern tendencies!

The Queen's Head has beams galore and separate public and saloon bars, as in the old days. The building is around 350 years old and when the customers have all gone it is said that ghosts lurk. It is a friendly, comfortable place, though, and visitors are made welcome. The real ales are Greene King IPA and Abbot and Tolly Cobbold Winter Ale in season, with guest beers which are changed every two months. Draught Dry Blackthorn cider is also available. A celebrated steak and kidney pie is on the menu (home-made) and at the right time of year you can sample game pies. There is a pleasant garden to the rear to be enjoyed whenever the weather permits and

the French game of pétanque is popular here. The hours of opening are from 11.30 am to 3.30 pm and 6 pm to 11 pm on Monday to Friday, 12 noon to 11 pm on Saturday and 12 noon to 10.30 pm on Sunday.
Telephone: 01621 860262.

How to get there: Tolleshunt D'Arcy can be reached from Maldon, travelling north-east, or from Colchester, travelling south, in both cases along the B1026. If you are approaching from the A12 come off at Kelvedon and take the B1023 through Tiptree.

Parking: At the pub, but please ask permission to leave your car while you walk.

Length of the walk: 5 miles. Map: OS Landranger 168 Colchester and The Blackwater area (inn GR 930121).

A magnificent walk on tracks and field paths, in sight of the Blackwater Estuary for much of the way. Even the previous existence of the branch line from Kelvedon to Tollesbury has left this area little affected by the modern world.

The Walk

Leaving the pub, turn left along North Street (going south!) and at the corner by the Red Lion turn left, passing a series of houses, some quite old. Probably the oldest is marked 'Spring Farm 1665', a very pretty building. The road bends to the right and soon you will turn left by a concrete footpath sign. Keep on your line to reach some garden gates. Here turn left and walk with a fence on your right and a ditch on your left. At the field corner turn right onto a track. After less than 100 yards turn left over a narrow plank bridge which crosses a ditch. Follow this field edge until you reach a stile on your right. Cross this, going through a grassy area at Guisnes Court. Soon a diversion takes you over a stile to the right and you carry on your original direction south-east, with distant views of the

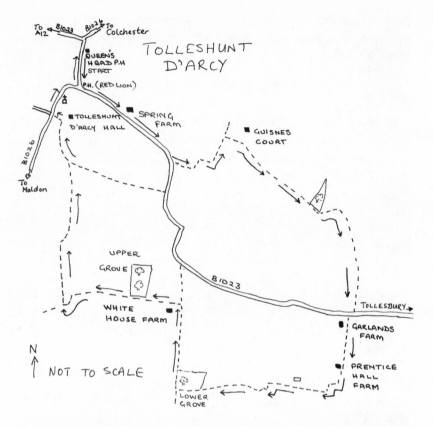

TOLLESHUNT D'ARCY

NOT TO SCALE

Blackwater. You pass the houses at Guisnes Court and follow the track to right and left to continue on a broad way between the fields.

After passing a strip of woodland follow the signs to right and left, then take the path south towards the Tollesbury road. Before you do that look for the splendid views north-east over the Old Hall Marshes to West Mersea. These are especially fine after the harvest and in the winter but may be partially obscured by the crops in the summer.

At the road turn right and soon left by Garlands Farm, then walk past Prentice Hall round a right and left bend. At a concrete footpath sign turn right. Carry straight on over a track by a yellow arrow and then across a railed bridge. Turn left

Tolleshunt D'Arcy church.

for a few yards to cross a plank bridge. Here turn right up the hill, with a hedge on your right, to walk by Lower Grove to a road. Turn right for ½ mile to White House Farm. Take the route left here through the farm steading (Upper Grove is on your right). Rounding a bend, turn right at a waymark, with a line of trees on your left. At the field end turn right and left round some trees and continue over a railed bridge. Here the definitive line continues north over the field but an alternative route laid out by the farmer goes left by the stream and right up a track, with the hedge on your right, to reach a broad way. Turn left and follow this track right and left to the Maldon road. Turn right towards the church (which is worth a visit). Now follow the road for a few minutes back to the Queen's Head.

16 Fordham Heath
The Cricketers

A heath is defined as a bare, flat waste tract of land, usually covered with low shrubs. Though abounding with commons, Essex seems to have very few heaths. Navestock Heath near Brentwood is one and Fordham Heath, which, incidentally, lies in the parish of Eight Ash Green rather than Fordham, is another. For Fordham Heath to be thought of as a waste tract of land is not very fair – it is most attractive and must be valued highly by the residents nearby.

The Cricketers lies opposite the fine cricket ground which takes up part of the heath. In this case we know the name of the pub relates to the local game for until recent times the pub was called the Star. It is a fairly large house, owned by Greene King, with a rebuilt lounge bar and a restaurant. Only 2 to 3 miles from central Colchester, this is a popular place for a meal or a drink and a snack. The real ales are Greene King IPA and Abbot, and sometimes the seasonal beers which are a

An impressive home, seen along the route.

recent feature of Greene King's repertoire can be sampled here. The cider on tap is Red Rock. There is an extensive menu in the restaurant and you can also choose from a wide range of bar food. If you have the time on a Sunday for a three course roast lunch, you will not be disappointed. The Cricketers has a large garden where children are welcome, with accompanying adults, as well as in the restaurant. The pub is open from 12 noon to 3 pm every day and in the evening from 6 pm to 11 pm on Monday to Saturday and 6.30 pm to 10.30 pm on Sunday.

Telephone: 01206 240666.

How to get there: From the A12 west of Colchester, exit to the north on the A604. Continue on this road past a large roundabout. Just beyond a post office turn right and after about ½ mile you will find the Cricketers on the right.

Parking: At the pub there is a large car park. However, please get permission to leave your car there while taking the walk.

Length of the walk: 3¾ miles. Map: OS Landranger 168 Colchester and The Blackwater area (inn GR 947263).

There are lots of interesting features on this route, which travels around a small part of the beautiful Colne valley, in the parishes Eight Ash Green, West Bergholt and Fordham. The circuit passes Cook's Mill, Cook's Hall and Great Porter's Farm, with a stretch along one of the finest parts of the Essex Way. You must do this walk!

The Walk
From the pub turn right, walking if you like on the edge of the cricket ground on the heath. At a T-junction go straight on, that is north at Cook's Mill North Cross road. As you descend the Colne valley the surrounding countryside is very beautiful. On the lower ground turn right towards Cook's Mill through an avenue of trees. Soon cross the river Colne and bear left after passing the house at Cook's Mill. A pillbox is nearby from the Second World War. At the house gates take the middle of three paths, which runs north towards farm buildings ahead (ignore a stile on your left). At the end of the field pass a derelict cottage and turn left at a T-junction of paths.

You are now on the route of the Essex Way, and at one of its prettiest points. Continue in the farmyard, past an oil storage tank, to cross a stile with an Essex Way sign. You are walking westwards some yards to the north of the river Colne, in a tranquil area where sheep may safely graze! Cross a stream and fork left. Up on the hill to the right stands Fordham church, seemingly guarding our way, as it has done for 600 years. At a field corner turn left then right, crossing a waymarked stile followed by a plank bridge. Along this way we expect a bridge over the river but at present our route

76

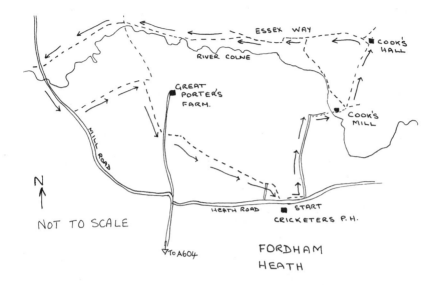

continues to a road (Mill Road).

Turn left, ignoring Essex Way signs, and cross the river on the road. In a few yards (about 150) look for a stile on your left. Over the stile, the route is usually just about visible underfoot, but in any case aim to the left of a bushy-topped tree. At the top of the slope turn right to pass Great Porter's Farm to your left. The waymark situation on this path is improving, and at the crossing hedge turn left to a stile by the farm road. Cross to another stile and walk along a field edge, with a hedge on your left. After a few yards bear right across the field corner, heading south-east for ½ mile to a short green lane by a house, then an access road to Heath Road.

Cross the road and turn left across the heath to the Cricketers. Like our dog, who frequently wanted to continue a walk when we thought we'd finished, you may well wish to go on exploring this lovely heathland. Feel free!

17 Boxted
The Wig and Fidgett

The Wig and Fidgett, as its name implies, has a legal connection. The present building is about 100 years old. The previous Wig and Fidgett, on the same site, was an alehouse and also a courthouse in which all the local cases were tried. The wig refers to that worn by a judge, while a fidgett is the base on which a wig rests when not on the head of the said legal gentleman. This pub was at one time a staging post in the process of passing smuggled brandy from Harwich to Colchester and in those days a wig and fidgett were displayed in the window. If the wig was on the fidgett, it would be safe to pass, if not then beware!

All this heady history cannot disguise that this is a friendly inn with an established local trade. Real ales are represented by the popular Greene King IPA, while Scrumpy Jack is on tap for cider fanciers. The menu of well-prepared, simple food provides value for money, the English Breakfast – egg, bacon, sausage, tomato, mushrooms, beans and two slices of bread and butter – being a particularly good buy. In the dessert line, pineapple meringue or spotted dick and custard, for example, are both tempting. There is a room in the pub which can accommodate children, and a large garden, for adults as well, of course! The Wig and Fidgett also has a field for caravans. The opening hours are 11 am to 3 pm and 6 pm to 11 pm on Monday to Saturday and 12 noon to 3 pm and 7 pm to 10.30 pm on Sunday.

Telephone: 01206 272227.

How to get there: Make for the centre of Colchester and drive north on the A134. From the station area drive under the railway lines and after about a mile fork right, signposted to Boxted. This road is very straight and hence it is called Straight Road. After going over the A12 trunk road you will reach the pub in 1¾ miles, on your right.

Parking: At the pub. The landlord is happy for you to leave your car while you go on the walk but it might be courteous to let him know that this is what you propose to do.

Length of the walk: 4 miles. Map: OS Landranger 168 Colchester and The Blackwater area (inn GR 001317).

A very beautiful walk with a visit to a fine church in Boxted and magnificent views, first of the pond at Pond House and later, more extensively, of the Stour valley and the Naylands.

The Walk
Outside the pub turn right along Straight Road. The traffic here is not frequent but by the nature of its 'straightness' it's fast, so take care. Ignore a public footpath sign on the left and soon join a grass verge. About 250 yards from the pub, at a concrete public footpath sign, turn left along a pretty track. Pass through a metal kissing-gate and continue along a visible

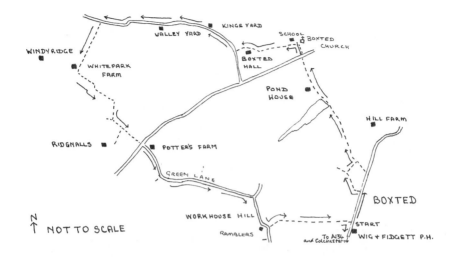

path in a pasture field. At the field corner do not cross the stile but turn right, with a hedge on your left, to a kissing-gate in the next corner. Pass through this gate and turn left near a sign telling us that 'Dogs kill sheep'. Take this good path, with a hedge on the left. Over to your right is Hill Farm. The reason for the name soon becomes apparent as you reach a deep descent to a large pond. Go through another kissing-gate then pass the east end of the pond and a large dwelling named Pond House. Join the drive from the house and walk on to the road at Boxted church, by a black public footpath sign.

Cross the road and go down a lane marked 'Boxted School'. In a few yards the route turns left at a public footpath sign but you may wish to take a look at the environs of the school and the church. Having done so, take the nice path west alongside the burial ground towards Boxted Hall. This grass path is in excellent condition, not muddy and a good metre wide. You are now on the Essex Way (briefly) and so follow the waymarks round the back of the hall out to a lane.

Turn right and soon there are splendid views of Suffolk over the Stour, specifically of Nayland church in the valley and Stoke by Nayland church on the ridge. You will encounter little traffic on this lane and you pass Kings Yard, then Valley

81

The pond with its eponymous house beyond.

Yard. Turn left at a black footpath sign, walking uphill to Whitepark Farm. Just over to the right is a large house named Windyridge. At Whitepark Farm walk past the house and immediately turn left along a track, which leads you downhill.

Before leaving the Stour valley look back at the magnificent scene of the Naylands for a final time. Cross over a stream and when you arrive at a facing hedge turn right uphill, changing sides on the way so that the hedge is now on your right. Do not enter a hedged lane leading to Ridgnalls, instead turn left across a field on a reinstated path to a road at a black footpath sign. Cross the road and continue down a little street named Green Lane. Again, there is rarely any traffic this way and walking conditions are easy. You come to a cluster of houses. At a T-junction turn right, directed to Workhouse Hill. Climb up this hill and turn left at a footpath sign, just after a house on the right aptly named the Ramblers. Follow this wide path between fields to the road at a footpath sign. Turn right along the road for just a few yards to the Wig and Fidgett.

⑱ Brightlingsea
The Anchor Hotel

The town's name probably comes from Brightlings Island, indeed the area is marked on old maps as an island. Long ago Brightlingsea was a Cinque Port member, being affiliated to Sandwich, and the inhabitants were consequently exempt from serving on juries or in the militia. There has been quite an amount of shipping here over the years, though the port is now more the centre of the oyster fisheries. At high tide the quay is a lovely scene with trim yachts and sturdy smacks stretched seaward – and when the yachts are sailing it is said that the heart of the Essex man leaps up!

The Anchor pub stands right on the waterside, in a slightly ornate building which has the look of a hostelry well used to being at the centre of things. The licensee is a lady who is dedicated to providing food and drink of the best quality – all day. All types of pub grub are available, but the jewel in the crown is the fish that her husband catches personally each day from his boat. Fresh cod in the finest thin batter is a delight. The real ales are Adnams Bitter and Extra with, usually, Mauldons Bitter as well. Olde English cider is also on tap. The opening hours are 11 am to 11 pm (10.30 pm on Sunday).

Telephone: 01206 302035.

How to get there: The most straightforward directions are to leave the A120 on the A133. At the first roundabout turn right for Colchester and then go left on the B1029 for Thorrington and Brightlingsea. Stay on this road into the town centre and at Victoria Place turn right down New Street. Pass left along Waterside to reach the Anchor Hotel.

Parking: At the hotel or in the free car park behind. If leaving your car at the Anchor, remember to ask permission at the bar before setting out on your walk.

Length of the walk: 5¼ miles. Map: OS Landranger 168 Colchester and The Blackwater area (inn GR 086163).

The going is fairly easy on this delightful walk and the sights and sounds are well worth every step. A day in Brightlingsea is as good as a short holiday.

The Walk

Leave the pub and turn away from the harbour past the harbourmaster's office. Through the car park, walk up Tower Street for about 100 yards to turn right into Lime Street. At the corner turn right again, into a footpath. Follow this on the field edge to reach the sea wall going east. This part of the walk skirts Brightlingsea Creek and is known as the Rope Walk. At a point where there is a house with boatworks turn inland on a broad track, then at the corner turn sharp left to some old cottages on Mill Street. Turn right along this road for a few yards to take a path to the left at a black public footpath sign and stile.

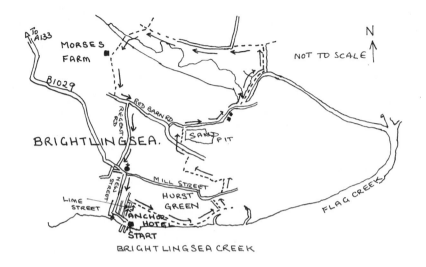

BRIGHTLINGSEA CREEK

Walk across the middle of the field to another stile and turn left on a path to the corner of houses ahead. Both paths here get you forward in the right direction but follow the one on the right, away from the garden walls, for better views. Pass through a gap in the hedge and turn right at the next corner to reach a road. Turn left along this for 150 yards to turn right into a path opposite Granville Way at a concrete public footpath sign.

Go along this path high above a very large pond, then turn right at a T-junction of paths and walk about 500 yards to a large house. Bear to your left with a yellow arrow and, after passing the house, two more arrows lead you to a stile, which in turn leads to a second stile. Turn right and then left over a third stile. Now climb the sea wall and follow it for 750 yards, going north-east. Look for a stile and bridge with a yellow arrow down to your left. Climb down from the wall and negotiate this stile, walking up the field to the far corner on your right. Turn left along the fence and, continuing in the same direction, cross two stiles to the corner of a white road.

Carry on past an old barn on your left to another stile.

A smartly-painted figurehead adorns the harbourmaster's office at Brightlingsea.

Having crossed this, bear left to cross streams by way of two plank bridges and a concrete bridge. Now get over the next stile into a hedged lane leading to Morses Farm, a very appealing group of buildings with what appears to be a style of farming from a bygone era. At a black footpath sign turn left over a field and walk due south over a field path to a stile near some industrial buildings. A paved path leads to a road (Red Barn Road).

Turn left for 200 yards and cross into Regent Road. In this there are many houses from earlier in this century, as well as evidence of Brightlingsea at play – including the cricket club and tennis club. When the road veers to the right go down Queen Street to the centre of the town. Turn left and right down New Street to reach Waterside where the Anchor Hotel awaits.

⑲ Bradfield
The Strangers Home Inn

Bradfield has grown up at the highest point of this comparatively low-lying country in north-east Essex, at a crossroads where the Harwich road is joined by a minor road from Bradfield Heath. It is there that we find the church and the pub, less than ½ mile from the Stour Estuary, the village enjoying views of the water. On the southern side of Bradfield Heath is a handsome moated house, Bradfield Hall, with a 400 year old wing. Here was born Sir Harbottle Grimstone, who became Speaker of the House of Commons in 1660 and was sent to Holland to recall Charles II, to whom he delivered the official speech of welcome in Parliament.

The Strangers Home Inn, which is about 100 years old, caters mainly for local villagers in the winter, with a much larger clientele in the summer, including visitors staying in the pub's camping and caravan site in a large field towards the

Stour. This is a friendly, welcoming hostelry at any time of the year. Food is served every day – the usual sandwiches and bar snacks, as well as more substantial dishes of fillet or rump steak, Strangers vegetable and ham soup and steak and kidney pie. The real ales are Boddingtons Mild and Bitter, Bass and Flowers Original. You will find that the opening hours vary according to the season. In winter the inn is open all week from 12 noon to 3 pm and 7 pm to 11 pm (10.30 pm on Sunday). In summer the times are 11 am to 11 pm on Monday to Saturday and 12 noon to 10.30 pm on Sunday.

Telephone: 01255 870304.

How to get there: Take the eastern section of the A120 off the A12 north of Colchester, signposted to Harwich. East of Horsley Cross there is a roundabout signposted to Manningtree and Bradfield. At Bradfield Heath a road to the right is signed to Bradfield and you will come to the pub after about a further mile.

Parking: Park at the pub, but please ask at the bar before leaving your car while you walk.

Length of the walk: 3¾ miles. Map: OS Landranger 168 Colchester and The Blackwater area (inn GR 143308).

A marvellous walk incorporating parts of the Essex Way. In addition there is a fine section along the shore of the Stour as it widens to the sea.

The Walk

Emerging from the pub, turn right to the village hall and go right along Mill Lane. Pass an anonymous, though new, burial ground on your right and allotments on your left. After going alongside a thicket the road bends left and we leave it, turning to the right at a black public footpath sign, to follow part of the Essex Way.

Cross through a hedge by a post and arrow. Hereabouts the

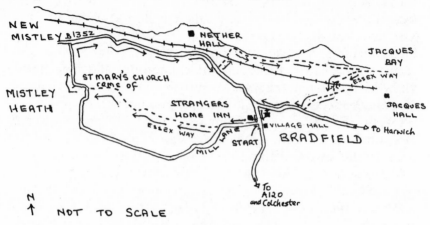

RIVER STOUR

NEW
MISTLEY B1352   NETHER
                       HALL   JACQUES
                                                 BAY
        ST MARY'S CHURCH   ESSEX WAY
MISTLEY -come of
HEATH   STRANGERS   JACQUES
                       HOME INN   HALL
              ESSEX WAY   To Harwich
                         START   VILLAGE HALL
                    MILL LANE   BRADFIELD

N
↑   NOT TO SCALE

To
A120
and Colchester

path has been slightly realigned and a broad strip is now left
between the crops. On reaching a wooded area, pass a pond
on the left and cross a plank bridge leading to a stile by a
bungalow, onto a road. Turn right, passing the few remains of
St Mary's church. At a T-junction turn right along the B1352
leading to Harwich, watching out for traffic. The road twists
and turns. On your left is the Stour and, nearer, the railway.
You pass close to a level crossing and then in 100 yards turn
left off the road, under the railway, to the waterside.

If the tide is out a fine path follows the shore below the sea
wall, otherwise the path on the wall is the answer. Here you
can enjoy all the sights and bird calls of the sea. After barely ¾
mile, spot a post with arrows and an Essex Way sign which
points back to your right across a field to a tunnel under the
railway. Through the tunnel, continue in the south-west
direction for 600 yards, crossing a kissing-gate and then a stile
onto the Harwich road. Turn right and walk about 300 yards
to reach Bradfield church and the Strangers Home.

The church is well worth a look inside. It has an interesting
pulpit in which the Georgian carpenters reused older carved
panels. There is a bell of over 600 years old, pre-dating its
tower, which was constructed in the 16th century, its cheerful

builders giving each of its four faces a row of seven jovial heads.

Places of interest nearby

If you would like to make a complete day out of it, you could visit *Mistley Place Park* which is just up the road, to the east of Manningtree, on the B1352. The accent here is very much on animals. The park incorporates an animal rescue and environmental centre with over 1,000 creatures on show. Somewhere in the 25 acres which comprise the park, there are rescued farm and domestic animals including horses, ponies, goats, sheep, turkeys, geese, chickens and rabbits. In addition, there are meadows, paddocks, woodland and nature trail habitats for visitors to explore. There is also a holly bush maze and a gift shop and tearooms. It is open throughout the year and offers much reduced admission charges for children under 4 years (free!) and for senior citizens. Mistley Place Park is at New Road, Mistley, opposite the church. For further information, telephone 01206 396483.

Thorpe-le-Soken
The Bell Hotel

Thorpe-le-Soken, north of Clacton, has an interesting church with a fine red tower and, some say, the grave of Jack the Ripper in its churchyard. Among the charming old buildings in the village are Abbey House, and its near neighbour, the 15th-century Bell. The latter is certainly a joy to visit and also offers five letting rooms – ideal if you wish to stay longer in this part of Essex, perhaps doing the other nearby walks in this book at the same time. The inn, we are told, has its own ghost, about which there is a story. The Reverend Henry Gough, who was vicar of Thorpe until he died in 1774, married Kitty Canham from Beaumont Hall but she did not love him and was unable to endure the tedium of life in a remote vicarage. She ran off to London, met Lord Dalmeny and spent four years travelling about Europe with him until she became ill at Verona. Realising she was dying, and not able to speak, she wrote down her confession and a request that she be buried at Thorpe. The noble lord brought her body back to the village and the Reverend Gough, though at first furious, perceived his lordship's devotion to Kitty and followed the coffin at his side to its resting place in the western corner of the north aisle. This was not the end of the matter, however, for Kitty's ghost is said to appear in the inn at dead of night.

Unusually, the entrance to the Bell is up a set of steps and one walks into a well-timbered room which contains the bar before, intriguingly, going down into what is now the restaurant. The tables in the bar are traditional wrought-iron legs and bases with circular mirror tops. Now owned by the Pubmaster group, the inn is run with skill and certainly some sophistication. Food is served throughout the opening hours. There is a varied bar menu with, for example, triple-deck club sandwiches, croque monsieur, calamari and rack of barbecue ribs served with corn on the cob and garlic bread. The 'all day breakfast' consists of two eggs, grilled bacon, pork sausages, tomatoes and fried bread, accompanied by tea or coffee. The restaurant offers an à la carte menu. As for drinks, the real ales are Greene King IPA, Flowers Original and Tetley Bitter. Outside there is a pleasant garden with a close view of the church. The bar times are 11 am to 11 pm on Monday to Saturday and 12 noon to 10.30 pm on Sunday.

Telephone: 01255 861394.

How to get there: From the A120 east of Colchester join the A133, signposted to Clacton. Leave this road on the B1033, going through Weeley to Thorpe-le-Soken. The Bell Hotel is down the High Street near the church, on the right, with the car park on the left.

Parking: Park in the pub car park, but please check at the bar before leaving your car there while you walk.

Length of the walk: 5¼ miles. Map: OS Landranger 168 Colchester and The Blackwater area (inn GR 179223).

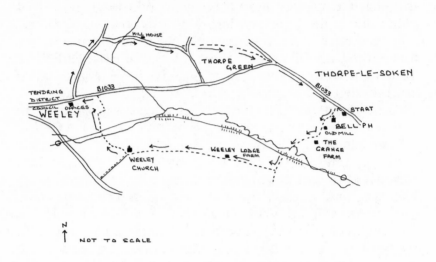

This route belies the impression that the Tendring district is all flat. There are sections of great beauty on this circuit to Weeley church and Thorpe Green and, together with the sights of old Thorpe around the church, they make this walk from the ancient Bell a must!

The Walk

Turn left after descending the steps from the Bell and then turn left into the churchyard by a black public footpath sign. Walk past the church and turn right through a metal kissing-gate to a broad track. Turn left, passing the Old Mill on your left and a very pretty thatched cottage on your right. Soon a yellow arrow beckons you onto a farm track heading for The Grange Farm. Keep on past the farm buildings to reach the Holland Brook. A good hand-railed bridge permits you to cross this and the path continues under power lines to a level crossing onto a grass track.

The track leads to the corner of a broad farm track. Here turn right and walk towards Weeley Lodge Farm. Beyond this you come to Weeley church, standing proudly by the two large ponds. Just past the church turn right along a wide track to reach the railway line again, with two kissing-gates on either side of the level crossing. Walk for some yards through a hedged track and, on emerging, immediately turn right at a fork in the paths and follow the footpath sign across the field. Turn right with another black footpath sign and finally left with another. Climb over a stile and walk, with a hedge on your left, to take two metal gates to a road with a stile and a concrete public footpath sign.

Turn left along the main road for 250 yards. Turn right opposite Tendring District Council Offices, along a lane signposted to Tendring, with interesting houses to be seen. Just after passing a wood turn right on a pretty little road marked 'no through way'. Cross the brook on a footbridge, continuing on a road to Hill House. Though motorised traffic may not use this road, it appears that the owners permit walkers to pass. This little grouping of road, trees and houses is very pretty. Go on beyond the house to join a path on the left by a concrete public footpath sign, crossing a field to another footpath sign. Over a lane, take the plank bridge by a footpath sign. Keep the hedge on your right to a bridge over the stream. Turn half-right and aim for a solitary oak tree in the hedge opposite. Through this, continue across the next field to the projecting corner of a large garden. On this corner is a sign marked 'footpath'. Keep on, with the garden hedge on your right. The accompanying house is palatial. Soon you come to Thorpe village green, which is impressive indeed.

Cross the green to a footpath sign and walk on the wide road past all the interesting houses and other sights of the village, finally coming to the car park of the Bell.